HELLO KITTY

and friends

The Christmas Present

TWO SPECIAL CHRISTMAS STORIES

HELLO KITTY
and friends

The Christmas Present
TWO SPECIAL CHRISTMAS STORIES

HarperCollins *Children's Books*

With special thanks to
Linda Chapman and Michelle Misra

First published in Great Britain by HarperCollins *Children's Books* in 2013

www.harpercollins.co.uk
1 3 5 7 9 10 8 6 4 2
ISBN: 978-000-751581-3

Printed and bound in England by Clays Ltd, St Ives plc.

MIX
Paper from
responsible sources
FSC˚ C007454

FSC™ is a non-profit international organisation established to promote
the responsible management of the world's forests. Products carrying the
FSC label are independently certified to assure consumers that they come
from forests that are managed to meet the social, economic and
ecological needs of present and future generations,
and other controlled sources.

Find out more about HarperCollins and the environment at
www.harpercollins.co.uk/green

Contents

MEET
HELLO KITTY
and friends

Hello Kitty

Mimmy

Tammy

Mama

Papa

Grandpa

Grandma

Fifi

Dear Daniel

·STORY ONE·

The Christmas Tree

Contents

Christmas Is Coming!

Hello Kitty crossed her arms and sat up as straight as she could as Miss Davey, her teacher, looked around the class. Hello Kitty was wishing **hard** that Miss Davey would call on her. Every day since the first of

December, Miss Davey had chosen one person

to go up to the front and open the next door of

the advent calendar.

Miss Davey's eyes settled on Hello Kitty and

she **smiled**. Today would be Hello Kitty's

turn! Hello Kitty jumped to her feet and hurried

to Miss Davey's desk. She found the little door

marked with the number '5' and opened it
carefully. What would the picture be?

It was a beautiful Christmas tree decorated
with coloured balls and tinsel. Miss Davey asked
Hello Kitty to carry the calendar round and
show it to the whole class. She hoped that the
class would make sure the school's very own
Christmas tree looked just as *beautiful*
by the end of the day.

They all nodded excitedly. Their class had

been picked to decorate the school Christmas

tree! It was going to

be delivered at

lunchtime and they

were going to get

out the decorations

and make it look

lovely and festive.

Hello Kitty felt

just **super** even

thinking about

it – she loved

Christmas! She loved everything about it, especially…

❄ Putting up decorations

❄ Singing carols

❄ Hanging up her stocking

And *PRESENTS*

of course!

Hello Kitty gave the advent calendar back to Miss Davey, who hung it on the wall. She told the class to use the last ten minutes before lunch to finish off the Christmas stories they were writing.

Hello Kitty sat back down with Dear Daniel, Fifi and Tammy. The four of them were such good friends that they had started their very own Friendship Club – they had meetings at each other's houses, made things, baked, had sleepovers and went on outings. It was **great**

fun! They also made up rules about friendship.

They had quite a few so far, like...

- Good friends are always there when you need them most.
- Good friends never need to show off to each other.
- Good Friends come in all shapes and sizes.

Hello Kitty picked up her pen, but she wasn't

ready to finish off her story just yet – she wanted

to talk about Christmas! She wished it wasn't

still twenty days away. That was **AGES!**

Tammy whispered that she was sure the time would fly by. There was so much to do! As well as having the tree to decorate, they would be doing all sorts of interesting things at school. Miss Davey had told them they were going to bake a chocolate cake called a Christmas

log, make Christmas cards for their parents, sew some mini Christmas stockings and learn some new Christmas songs.

Dear Daniel and Fifi nodded. And there was

their year group's Christmas play of course!

Hello Kitty felt a little leap of **excitement**.

She didn't know what the play was yet, but

she had volunteered to help organise it. She

was going to a meeting about it at lunchtime.

She really wanted to be the costume designer,

but even if she couldn't do the costumes, she

would be happy helping with anything at all. She

just wanted to be involved! Hello Kitty loved

organising things.

BRRRRRRRRING!

The lunch bell went.

Everyone put down their

pens but before they left, Miss

Davey reminded them that some of the older

years were doing a sponsored silence that day

in aid of PAWS, a local animal shelter, and she

didn't want anyone to disturb them or make

them talk. Miss Davey had got her dog Spot

from PAWS. The more money they raised the

better – there would be **lots** of animals in

the shelter at Christmas and the helpers there

needed money to buy food and blankets and

Christmas treats. It was a very good cause.

Everyone agreed not to disturb them and

then Miss Davey let them go for lunch. Hello

Kitty said goodbye to Fifi, Tammy and Dear

Daniel and hurried off to the library for her

meeting. Was she going to be able to help with

costumes? And what was the play going to be?

She simply couldn't *WAIT* to find out!

Exciting News

Hello Kitty sat down with eight other girls and boys. Her teacher Miss Davey was there with another teacher. Miss Davey would be organising all the acting, *singing* and dancing in the play, and the other teacher would be helping her.

Hello Kitty got her sparkly pink notepad out of her bag and her matching pen so she could make notes. She opened her pad up and wrote the heading:

THE CHRISTMAS SHOW

Oooh, she hoped she would be able to have something to do with the costumes!

Miss Davey was delighted they all wanted to help. She told them that she needed people to help paint the scenery and then move the

scenery during the actual play, and people to

organise the costumes and also the props – the

small things the actors would carry on stage

with them. She would also need someone to

remind the actors if they forgot their lines.

One of the other girls asked what the play

would be. Miss Davey

smiled. It was going to

be a **VERY**

Christmassy show.

They were going

be doing… The

Nutcracker!

28

Hello Kitty gasped in delight. She loved The Nutcracker. It was normally performed as a ballet, and Hello Kitty loved to dance! Miss Davey said there would definitely be some dancing in it, but they would be doing it as a play, with *singing*. It was about a girl called Clara who was given a wooden nutcracker on Christmas Eve. The nutcracker looked like a soldier. Her brother, Fritz, broke the nutcracker and Clara was very sad, but then at midnight the

Nutcracker came alive. After winning a fierce battle against the Mouse King, he whisked Clara away to The Land of Sweets and introduced her to amazing characters like the Sugar Plum Fairy. Clara had an amazing time before coming home just in time for Christmas with her family.

Hello Kitty's mind *raced* as everyone else started to talk about it. She could already see some of the costumes in her head. The Sugar Plum Fairy would wear pale pink – maybe a ballet tutu

and glittery top. Clara would be in a pretty white nightgown. Clara's little brother Fritz would wear shorts and a waistcoat…

Miss Davey **clapped** her hands to stop the excited chatter. It was time to decide who was going to do what!

Hello Kitty listened carefully as Miss Davey asked who would like to do the scenery. Almost everyone put up their hands.

Miss Davey wrote their names down and then asked who would like to do costumes. Hello Kitty nervously put up her hand. She was the **only one!**

Miss Davey smiled at her. Hello Kitty would be the costume designer! She felt like jumping up and down with joy. **Hooray!** She was so happy. Miss Davey said that some of the other teachers had volunteered to make the costumes, but Hello Kitty could design them. It would be a lot of work. But Hello Kitty didn't mind at all. Drawing clothes never felt like work to her!

They finished off deciding who was going to do what and then Miss Davey told them the meeting was over and they should go and have their lunch. The auditions were going to be the next morning. Anyone who wanted to have a main part needed to audition and then she and some other teachers would choose who would be just right for each part.

Hello Kitty pushed her notebook into her bag and hurried out of the library. She couldn't wait to find the others and tell them **all** about it!

Where would she find them?

She checked the lunch hall,

but they weren't in

there, so she ate

her lunch quickly

whilst making

some sketches

for costumes.

Afterwards, she set off to look for them again.

Suddenly, she had an idea – **of course!**

The Christmas tree! It was supposed to be

being delivered that lunchtime. Maybe they

were helping with that? Hello Kitty hurried to

the school reception area.

As she opened the doors, she saw her friends standing round the tree with Mrs Brown the headteacher, and some other school staff.

Hello Kitty frowned; everyone looked worried. *Whatever* was the matter?

And then she realised. The tree's branches

were all broken! It must have happened when it

was being delivered. There were pine needles all

over the floor too. *Oh no!* What were

they going to do? They couldn't

decorate a tree which didn't have any

branches. Mrs Brown was shaking

her head, saying that the school

couldn't afford another tree to replace the

broken one. This was terrible!

It looked like they weren't going to have a

Christmas tree in school this year after all.

Hello Kitty's Super Idea

Mrs Brown said she would call the caretaker

to come and take the tree away.

Dear Daniel spoke quickly; there had to be

something they could do, but Mrs Brown replied

sadly that the tree was too badly damaged for

them to even try to
use it. Hello Kitty hated
to see everyone looking so
miserable. But suddenly she had an idea.
Even if they didn't have a tree, they could
still get out the decorations and put them up
around the hall that afternoon, couldn't they?
It would make it look lovely and festive, even
without an actual Christmas tree.

Everyone cheered up. Mrs Brown thought
that was an *excellent* idea. There were
all sorts of things in the decorations box –
tinsel, paper chains, fairy lights and sparkly
ceiling decorations that hung down, and

she was sure that with a bit of work they could

make the hall look **great.** She went to her

office to fetch the key to the cupboard where

the Christmas decorations were kept.

Hello Kitty looked at some of the tree

branches on the floor. They could even use

those too – they could put them on the top of

the piano so that the hall would still smell of pine needles. Perfect!

The others agreed that Hello Kitty was right. It was sad not to have a tree but they could still make the hall look very festive for Christmas.

While they waited for Mrs Brown to come back with the decorations, Hello Kitty told them all about the play. They were **very excited** to hear that it was going to be the Nutcracker. Fifi definitely wanted to audition for a part – she wanted to be Clara! Hello Kitty did too, but she needed to think about whether she would audition or not, in

case she would be too busy designing

the costumes. Tammy said she

just wanted to be something

small. She didn't like the idea

of having to sing or dance

on her own on stage, but she

would be *happy* being in a

group. Dear Daniel

wanted to audition, too. He

didn't care what he was,

but he definitely wanted

to be in it. It sounded

like so much fun!

Hello Kitty told them that she was going

to be the costume designer. She started to

show them her sketches for the

costumes, but just

then Mrs Brown

returned with the

key, so they all went

into the hall to help

her get the boxes of

decorations out of the cupboard. She unlocked

the door. There were shelves inside holding four

massive cardboard boxes – but **why** were

there little shreds of paper all over the shelves,

and why did the boxes have holes in them?

Mrs Brown's forehead creased in concern. This didn't look good at all. She pulled a box out and looked inside – **Oh no!** Since last Christmas, a family of mice had made a nest in the cupboard and they had eaten through all the decorations!

Mrs Brown pulled all the decorations out of their boxes. The paper chains were shredded, and the tinsel was nibbled up so badly that the strands had fallen off the string. She held up one of the glittery ceiling decorations to look at

it more closely, and it fell apart in her hands!

The wire on the fairy lights had been chewed

through completely, and they were ruined too.

She quickly checked through all the boxes, but

the mice had nibbled everything!

This was a *disaster!* There was no

Christmas tree and now no decorations either.

Hello Kitty and her friends looked at each other

in dismay. If they couldn't decorate the hall, it wouldn't seem like Christmas in school at all.

Just then, two of the older girls came over to see what they were doing. They couldn't speak because of their sponsored silence but Mrs Brown explained what the problem was, and that it looked like the school wouldn't have **any** decorations for Christmas at all this year. The older girls looked very unhappy, but they still couldn't say anything. Mrs Brown explained to Hello Kitty and her friends that these two older girls and some of their friends had helped make the paper chains when they had started at the school. That year, they had held a decorating day where the whole school had spent the day helping out and making decorations.

As Hello Kitty looked at the older girls and their sad faces, all of a sudden, one of her **super, special** Hello Kitty ideas popped into her head!

She gasped. If Mrs Brown agreed, she had an

idea of how they could decorate the hall – and

get a new Christmas tree too!

Hard at Work

Hello Kitty quickly explained her idea to Mrs

Brown. What if their year had a decoration-

making afternoon the following day? They could

use materials from the school art cupboard and

bring things in from home and, even better, if

they got friends and family to sponsor them for something while they made the decorations, they could try and raise enough money to buy a new Christmas tree too!

Mrs Brown thought it was a *brilliant* plan. Would they do it as a sponsored silence like the older years, she asked? But Hello Kitty had an even better idea. Instead of a sponsored silence she thought they should have a sponsored sing instead – every time someone asked them something, they had to sing a reply! No one would be allowed to talk at all – only sing!

Mrs Brown *laughed*. She thought that sounded great! She would would print some sponsorship forms off for the year and have a word with Miss Davey. Would the Friendship Club help organise it all?

They beamed. **OF COURSE** they would!

Miss Davey was very sad to hear about the ruined decorations but she l♥ved the idea of the sponsored decoration-making afternoon the next day. She gathered up all the children in Hello Kitty's year to tell them about it. Hello Kitty waved at her twin sister, Mimmy, and then stood up at the front and told all of the classes about her idea.

Everyone was eager to help and they all volunteered to bring things in from home and get people to sponsor them to raise money. It would be *wonderful* if they could work hard enough to decorate the hall, and raise enough money to get a new tree too!

Fifi said she would ask her mum if there was any spare **glittery** material from the skating costumes she had made, and Mimmy suggested that she and Hello Kitty call in at the craft shop where their Mama bought things for making her jewellery. Maybe there would be some leftover bits and pieces they could have?

Fifi wrote a list on the whiteboard of useful things everyone could bring in the next day, while Dear Daniel asked people for ideas of things they could make. They decided on…

Paperchains

Snowflakes

Glittery holly leaves

Bunting with cut-outs of stockings

and Christmas puddings

Meanwhile, Tammy handed out

the sponsorship forms. Hello Kitty explained

that everyone would need to try and get people

to sponsor them for every hour that they

sang instead of speaking. The longer they

managed to do that for, the more money they

would all raise.

Everyone started to talk at once.

Miss Davey clapped her hands. Even though everyone was **excited**, she still had to tell them about the auditions for the play! They would be at lunchtime the next day. Everyone who wanted a part needed to sign up for an audition time. She told them the story of the Nutcracker and then played them some of the music, so that they could start preparing. The class

was buzzing with excitement by the end of

school. Auditions and a sponsored decoration-

making afternoon – they couldn't wait!

After school finished, Hello Kitty ran over

to where Mama White was waiting by the

school gates. She was *bursting* with news!

First though, she wanted to

ask Mama if the others

could come over for

a Friendship Club

meeting later that

afternoon. She

thought it would be **fun** to make mince pies and Christmas cupcakes and bring them into school for the decorating afternoon. Mama agreed, and as soon as the rest of the Friendship Club had spoken to their parents, it was all sorted. They would come round at five o'clock when Fifi had finished her ice-skating lesson and Dear Daniel had had his hair cut.

On the way home, Hello Kitty told Mama everything that had been happening, and Mimmy asked if they could stop at the craft shop. Mama took a look at her watch, and said

they could.

Mama parked the car and Mimmy and Hello

Kitty *ran* inside. They told the nice lady

behind the counter all about their sponsored

decorating afternoon at school, and asked if

there were any leftover items she didn't need

any more, that she would be happy to donate?

The lady **smiled**, and said that she would

be glad to help out. She bustled into the back

room and returned with two large boxes of

leftover glittery material, card, and red, gold

and green ribbon. Hello Kitty and Mimmy

squealed – it was **just** what they needed!

Then, the lady looked thoughtful. There should

be something about the sponsored decorating

day on the TV news! She mentioned that her

son was a reporter for the local news station,

and promised she would tell him all about it.

How exciting!

Hello Kitty and Mimmy thanked her and carried the boxes to the car. It was time to go home and get ready for the Friendship Club meeting!

At five o'clock, Dear Daniel, Fifi and Tammy

arrived and they all set to work in the kitchen,

baking. Hello Kitty put on some Christmas

songs and they all *sang* along as they worked.

Hello Kitty and Mimmy made pastry, rubbing

butter into the flour until it became all crumbly.

Meanwhile, Dear Daniel mixed the sugary icing

for the cupcakes, Fifi wiped some butter

around the mince pie tins and found the

rolling pin and cutters, while Tammy

mixed the cupcake ingredients together.

By the time they had finished, they were all covered in flour and the sink was overflowing with bowls and spoons. Mama had put the cakes and mince pies into the oven, and the kitchen smelled **l♥vely!**

While they washed up, Hello Kitty got everyone some lemonade. They were all very thirsty after their hard work! They had just finished washing the last bowl when the timer on the oven went off. Mimmy ran to fetch Mama and she took the mince pies and cupcakes out of the oven. *Mmmm...* they smelled delicious!

Once they were cool, they spread the icing on the cupcakes and decorated them with edible glitter and icing holly leaves. After that there was just one final thing to do – taste them!

They all agreed that both the cupcakes and the mince pies were completely **yummy**. They packed them into tins to take to school the next day, then it was time for everyone to go home.

As Hello Kitty put on her pyjamas that night she thought about school the next day — auditions for the play, making decorations, and only being allowed to sing and not speak. She had a feeling it was going to be the most fun school day **ever!**

5

Working Together

When Hello Kitty arrived at school the next day, she took the cupcakes and mince pies to the head office to keep them safe and then hurried to her classroom. The desks were already full! Everyone had brought in things to

make the Christmas
decorations, and
had brought their
sponsorship forms
back too, filled
with signatures.

Miss Davey

looked at all the sheets and **smiled** widely.
They wouldn't know quite how much money
they had raised until the sponsored sing
was over. She announced that they should
have a practice in their maths lesson
that morning – they would start
straightaway.

She went to the whiteboard to start the lesson, and started to teach them about fractions. She sang out all her instructions and then asked them a question. What was one quarter added to two quarters?

Everyone looked rather shy, so Hello Kitty took a deep breath and put up her hand. She sang out the answer – three quarters!

Everyone giggled as Miss Davey sang that it was the correct answer. Now, who could tell her what four fifths plus one fifth was?

That was a bit trickier, but everyone wanted to join in now! They **all** put up their hands and soon the class were singing out answers. There was a lot of giggling too. Hello Kitty didn't think she'd ever had such a fun maths lesson!

After break time, the auditions for the play started.

Miss Davey and some other teachers sat in the library and one at a time, all the girls and boys who wanted to be in the play read a piece from it. Hello Kitty and Fifi both auditioned for

Clara; Hello Kitty had thought about it for a **long** time, but had decided that even if she was going to be busy with the costumes, she still wanted to try out for the part! Dear Daniel auditioned for the part of the Mouse King, and the Nutcracker Soldier too.

Hello Kitty **enjoyed** reading the piece from the play, and then Miss Davey asked her to sing 'Jingle Bells.'

After everyone had finished, Miss Davey said that she and the other teachers would decide on the parts and put the cast list up in a few days time.

Hello Kitty and her friends hurried out. The auditions were over. Now it was time to think about decorations!

While the auditions had been going on, Mrs Brown had organised some of the other children to carry out all the decoration-making materials to the big hall. They had set out five tables where the different decorations could be made, and then there was one table which had everything needed for hanging them up around the hall.

Mrs Brown said she was looking forward to seeing the hall when it was all decorated. Hello Kitty looked at the clock. It was nearly twelve o'clock; **almost** time for them to start their sponsored singing! Mrs Brown got them all together, and everyone watched the clock together and counted down the last sixty seconds.

Five... four... three... two... one...

It was time to begin! From now on, everyone

had to sing and not speak.

All through lunch

and playtime and

then into the

afternoon, they

didn't speak,

only sang, as they

started to make their

decorations. It was **very** hard to remember,

but they were all determined to succeed! They

wanted to raise as much money as they could

for the new tree.

They had to sing to ask someone to pass the glue, and to ask someone to hold material so they could cut it out. And sing when they needed the tub of glitter.

Slowly, the pile of paper, card, ribbons and material started to change into decorations. There were **glittery** paper chains, bunting made out of cut-out stockings and Christmas puddings, and delicate snowflakes. Miss Davey started to hang things up. The hall was going to look amazing...

It was getting near to the end of school when Hello Kitty realised she had been so busy, she had almost **forgotten** about the cupcakes and mince pies in the head office! She went to Miss Davey and sang to her. Please could she go and fetch them? Miss Davey sang back that yes, that was fine.

Hello Kitty went to the office and found the tins of goodies. She was just about to go back to the hall when she saw a man and a woman

coming out of Mrs Brown's office. The woman was carrying a very **large** camera. What was going on?

Mrs Brown saw Hello Kitty and called her over to them. She said that the man and woman were from the local TV station. The lady from the craft shop had told her son the reporter about the decoration-making and sponsored singing,

and he wanted to film the children hard at work! If they were *lucky*, they would be on the local news programme that night. How exciting was that?

Even more exciting, Mrs Brown asked Hello Kitty if she would be happy to be interviewed by the reporter; he wanted to show someone telling him all about the day, by singing! Would that be OK?

There was only one answer. Hello Kitty sang out a big loud **YES!**

6

TV Stars!

That evening, all of the Friendship Club

and Mimmy sat with their parents around the

television at Hello Kitty's house, to watch the

local news.

The show started. There was some other

news first, and then **there** they were! The

programme showed their school hall with

everyone making decorations and singing to

each other, and then the picture changed –

there was Hello Kitty!

She was telling the

reporter all about the

broken Christmas tree and ruined decorations

and about the sponsored decoration-making

afternoon. She sang every word in the interview.

It sounded really **good!**

The others hugged her as they watched. Hello Kitty blushed pink; she felt very proud. The picture changed again and showed Miss Davey putting up the last of the decorations and everyone sharing the cakes and mince pies. There was a picture of Fifi offering the reporter a cake. He took a bite and said it was the **most** delicious thing he had ever tasted – with his mouth full! Fifi giggled. It was so funny seeing herself on TV!

The reporter spoke to the camera and said he *hoped* that all the children's hard work had paid off and that now the hall was decorated the girls and boys would find out if they had raised enough money to buy a Christmas tree for the school as well. They certainly deserved it…

There was a shot of all of Hello Kitty's class waving at the camera and then the programme returned to the newsreader in the studio.

Everyone in the room started to talk at once.

It had been **brilliant** seeing themselves

and their school on TV! Papa went to fetch

some drinks for the grown-ups and Hello Kitty

and Mimmy handed round the last of the mince

pies and cupcakes, as Fifi's dad asked when they

would find out if they had raised enough money

for a new Christmas tree.

Tammy replied that they were all taking in their sponsorship money the next day and Miss Davey was going to count it. Everyone crossed their fingers. Oh, they **REALLY** hoped they had raised enough!

When The Friendship Club got into school the next day, everyone was whispering to each other in excitement. What had happened? Just then, Tammy's twin brother Timmy ran

over to them... he had just heard the amazing

news that lots of people who had watched the

news report on TV had been donating money

as well! Together with all the sponsorship

money, it was enough for the school to buy a

big new tree and to have a large sum of money

left over to give to the animal shelter as well.

Hooray! How *perfect* was that?

Mrs Brown held a special school assembly to tell everyone the news. She said she was very proud of them all. Just a couple of days ago, it had seemed like the school's Christmas was going to be ruined, but because they had all worked together, everything had turned out brilliantly. Everyone had worked so hard, that they all deserved to give themselves three loud cheers.

Hip, hip, hooray! Hip, hip, hooray! HIP, HIP, **HOORAY!**

The Friendship Club all hugged each other with happiness. To celebrate, Hello Kitty thought they should have a new Friendship Club rule:

Good friends always work together to save the day!

Everyone REALLY liked that rule! But it wasn't quite complete, put in Dear Daniel. It needed one more line...

And good friends always have fun when they work together!

Hello Kitty thought about the last few days and grinned. That was definitely true for the Friendship Club! Now the school was ready for Christmas, and they had the Christmas show to look forward to as well. What could be better than that?

The end

Turn over the page for story two

The Christmas Show

·STORY TWO·
The Christmas Show

Contents

Letters to Santa

Hello Kitty looked across the school

playground to where her friends were hurrying

through the gates. Fifi was wearing a bright pink

fluffy hat with a bobble on the top, Tammy was

in a cosy white jacket and Dear Daniel had on

a red tasselled scarf. They'd have to take them off when they got inside, but Miss Davey had told them it was all right to wear home-clothes on their way into school while it was so **cold** outside.

Brrrrr. Hello Kitty wrapped her arms tightly around her body. It had turned really cold over the last few days. The clouds were very low in the sky that morning. Maybe, just maybe, it was going to snow in time for Christmas! She squeezed her eyes tight shut imagining snowball fights and building snowmen on Christmas Day.

How SUPER would that be?

Hello Kitty suddenly gave a little gasp as someone grabbed her around the waist and hugged her tight. She opened her eyes. It was Fifi! She was holding a piece of paper – her letter to Santa. The Friendship Club had all agreed to write them out last night and share them with each other that morning. They were going to write them out neatly and decorate them at Hello Kitty's house after school that afternoon. Hello Kitty looked down at Fifi's letter. It looked **a lot** shorter than hers!

Hello Kitty looked up again as Tammy and Dear Daniel came running over waving their letters too. They were about the same length as Fifi's. Oh dear! Hello Kitty's list was much longer than any of the others.

HELLO KITTY *and friends*

Dear Daniel started to read. He had asked for:

- **A bug finder**
- **A book about dinosaurs**
- **New football boots**
- **Felt tip pens**

Whereas Tammy wanted:

- A new detective book
- A diary
- A notebook for writing stories in
- A box of tricks

Fifi had drawn a picture of an ice-skater at the top of her list. She had only asked for four things too…

- Sparkly eye shadow
- Lip balm
- A book on ice-skating
- A new set of paints

But what about Hello Kitty? Blushing pink, Hello Kitty pulled her piece of paper out of her pocket. It was decorated around the edges with her costume ideas for the school play. She

started to read:

- Lip balms -Strawberry Surprise and Amazing Apple

- Sparkly hair clips

- Stickers

- A teddy bear

- Leg warmers

- Bubble Bath

Her list seemed to go on and on, and Hello Kitty went even pinker as she finally came to a stop. She knew she had to cut some of it, she told her friends, she just didn't know what! Thinking about Christmas presents was just so much *fun!*

She looked down at her list again. She really should take some things off... What about the lip balms? Maybe she didn't need two of those — but which one should she take off the list? She crossed out the Strawberry Surprise, but then she stopped

herself. She had nearly run out of that. Perhaps
the Amazing Apple should go instead, but she
really did love that one. Oh dear, whichever
should she choose? Hello Kitty wrinkled up her
brow, thinking hard.

At that moment, Hello
Kitty's twin sister Mimmy
came hurrying up to

them. Miss Davey was putting the cast list for

the Christmas show on the notice board that

morning! As soon as the bell went Mimmy

wanted to go inside and find out who was

playing which parts. Would they come with her?

The others chatted excitedly

about the show while

Hello Kitty kept

looking at her

list. It really was

VERY

difficult to figure

out what to take

off, and what to leave on...

BRIIIIIING!

The school bell went and the Friendship Club raced inside with Mimmy. Hello Kitty pushed her list into her pocket and followed them. As she reached the hall, she heard an excited buzz of chatter filling the air. People were crowding around the notice board. The cast list was up!

Hello Kitty felt her tummy *fizz*. Ever since she and her friends had auditioned, she had

been longing to know what part she would get.

And what about all her friends? She wriggled to

the front of the crowd to see.

The Cast List

The cast list had silver stars all over it

and the words The Nutcracker at the top.

Dear Daniel and Tammy were pointing at it

excitedly, and everyone who had auditioned

was whispering and smiling at each other. Hello

Kitty scanned it quickly. Tammy was a dancer in the Land of the Sweets. Timmy, Tammy's brother who was in Mimmy's class, was going to be playing Clara's little brother. Hello Kitty looked further down the list. Dear Daniel

was the Nutcracker soldier – a really **big part!** Susie in Mimmy's class was the Sugar Plum Fairy. So who was going to be Clara?

Hello Kitty's eyes came to rest on the name.

Fifi! Fifi had the main part!

It was **brilliant** news, but Hello Kitty

still felt a little disappointed. As pleased as she

was for her friend, a tiny part of her had hoped

that she might get the part of Clara as well as

being the costume designer. She looked further

down the list to where she and five others were listed as mice servants to the Mouse King. At least she had a *dancing* part, even if she wouldn't be singing. Hello Kitty knew that it made sense that she had a small part — after all, being the costume designer as well meant she wouldn't have much time for learning lines at all. So it really was much better this way!

Hello Kitty took a deep breath and put a smile on her face, as she turned to her friends and congratulated Fifi.

Fifi beamed. She really was very excited. So excited that for once, Fifi didn't know what to say! She had never imagined that she would get the main part, but Hello Kitty, Dear Daniel and Tammy all told her it made perfect sense. She was **brilliant** at singing and because of all the ice-skating that she did, she was very good at dancing too.

Ice-skating!

Fifi clapped her hand over

her mouth. She had

forgotten all about

that. She had a big

competition coming

up – the same week as

the Christmas play. However

would she manage to practise for them both?

Her friends told her that she would be just

fine. And besides, they could help! They would

practise the dance routines and the lines

together after school. They could even make

a start that afternoon at their Friendship Club

meeting. Hello Kitty linked her arm through her

Fifi's. It would be SO much fun!

Later that afternoon, as the Friendship Club

practised the opening scene of the Nutcracker

at Hello Kitty's house, Mama

came in carrying a jug

of lemonade and a

plate of chocolate

brownies. Yum!

The Friendship

Club WERE

hungry!

Mama stopped to watch as Dear Daniel, as

the nutcracker soldier, spun Fifi as Clara

around the floor before they stopped for a

drink. Mama smiled, and said that they were

doing so well! But she thought that maybe they

had done enough practising for one day; it was

probably time they took a break. The Friendship

Club agreed as they munched on the chocolate

brownies. But **what** would they do? They all decided to use the next hour before their parents came to pick them up to write out their letters to Santa neatly. Hello Kitty felt herself blush a little. She still hadn't managed to make hers any shorter! She pulled out a big box of craft materials and pens and glue that they could use to decorate their letters. In the box there were:

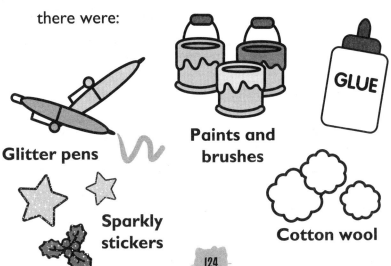

Glitter pens

Paints and brushes

GLUE

Sparkly stickers

Cotton wool

As Mama left the room, the Friendship Club

set to work. They wrote out their lists and

started to decorate them.

Tammy started with

the cotton wool, and

SOON she had

made a big snow-

scene to go around

her four items.

Fifi was painting a

snowman and adding silvery

sparkly stickers to look like snowflakes! Dear

Daniel was colouring in a picture of a Christmas

tree on his list. Hello Kitty was working on a

design for the Mouse King's costume for the Christmas play instead. She couldn't start to decorate her list until she had decided what she was going to cut…

Thoughtfully, she sucked on the end of her pencil and started to cross things off her list, before putting them back on again. She just couldn't choose what she wanted the most on her list. She looked over her shoulder. **Help!** Everyone else had nearly finished theirs.

Fifi started to wash out her paint brushes. Her list was done. Then Tammy and Dear Daniel said they were finished too, and Tammy suggested they all play a game of hide and seek

in the time left! Hello Kitty **knew** that she shouldn't really join in when she still had her letter to Santa to finish. But she wasn't enjoying it without knowing what to take off – she would finish it later.

She pushed her letter under a pile of cotton wool and ribbons and jumped to her feet. If the others wanted to hide, she would be it! Covering her eyes, she started to count.

3

Practice Makes Perfect

The next day at school was very busy, as was

the one after that. Hello Kitty's class seemed

to be spending all their time rehearsing their

lines for the play, painting scenery, and learning

dances and songs. Hello Kitty had finished all

the designs for the costumes and the teachers who had volunteered were *busy* making them. Mama had offered to come in and help too, and when Hello Kitty had time free from rehearsing she went to the teacher's rooms to help them. And she and Mama even carried on sewing at home!

Fifi was worried about learning her lines. She

had so many! Hello Kitty had offered to help but there was never any time at school.

So she had arranged to go and watch Fifi's skating lesson that afternoon so that they could practise *together* afterwards.

Fifi's mother collected them outside the school gates and drove them to the ice rink. As Fifi went off to change, Hello Kitty made her way over to the seats around the edge. She began to read through the scene Fifi wanted to

practise, murmuring the lines under her breath.
It was the part where Clara woke and found
the Mouse King in her room. He was fighting
the nutcracker and Clara had to stop him by
throwing her slipper at him. Hello Kitty couldn't
stop herself from **smiling** at the scene
as she mouthed the words. But now Fifi was
coming on to the ice...

Fifi waved across before gliding forward on one skate, her leg held out gracefully behind her. Hello Kitty could see how good Fifi was as she picked up speed and spun and pirouetted across the ice. It wasn't just about practice. Fifi was really talented! Finally, when Fifi's routine came to an end, she came over to join Hello Kitty, who held the script up. Should they start practising? But Fifi was tired. She wasn't sure that she felt much like practising now. Couldn't they just go for a hot chocolate instead, she asked hopefully?

Hello Kitty smiled. Of course they could!

Over the next few days, Hello Kitty tried to help Fifi with her lines as much as she could. But Fifi was so busy practising her skating before and after school there wasn't much time, no matter **how** much they tried to squeeze in. The competition was really important to Fifi. Hello Kitty read the scenes so many times when she was waiting for Fifi to come off the ice that she

began to know the words better than Fifi did!

Fifi **promised** she would start to

learn the script properly just as soon as her

competition was over. But the competition was

on Saturday, and then there would be just three

days until the play... Hello Kitty felt very worried

for her. Would three days be enough time for

Fifi to learn her lines *properly?* She

really hoped so!

4

Disaster Strikes!

Fifi waved to her friends from where she was

sitting at the side of the ice rink with her coach.

It was Saturday – the day of the ice-skating

competition – and it was just about to begin.

Hello Kitty was sitting with Tammy and Dear

Daniel. They had all come along to support Fifi.

It was chilly beside the ice and Hello Kitty felt

a wave of butterflies flood through her

tummy. After all the practising, she hoped that

Fifi would do well!

The first competitor was just coming on

to the rink. She was dressed in a pretty pink

leotard and tights, and a short silky pink skirt

that flared out around her.

Hello Kitty

loved the

outfits on everyone she could see. She watched as the graceful skater glided forwards before going into a **spin**, turning round and round on the spot. Hello Kitty watched closely, and soon the music came to an end.

The skater came off the ice and her scores were held up. Now another girl, in a costume made to look like black and red flames, was making her way on to the ice. Hello Kitty watched as she spun and jumped. She leaped really high, but she had two falls. One competitor followed another, their scores flashing up on the scoreboards when they had

finished their routines. Fifi was the last to skate
and finally, it was her turn. Hello Kitty crossed
her fingers as Fifi skated on to the ice and took
up her starting position – one leg behind the
other, hands and eyes down, her white costume
$glittering$ in the light. There was a long
pause while everyone waited in silence and then
the beautiful music began.

Fifi skated backwards, her legs crossing over on the ice as she got faster and faster, preparing for the first jump. Hello Kitty held her breath as Fifi **jumped** into the air, spinning twice over the ice, her arms held tight to her chest. She landed on one leg with the other held out behind her. She hadn't even wobbled!

Hello Kitty felt a rush of relief but there was no time to relax! Fifi was already skating on, picking up speed again before she

turned into a fast spin on the spot, one of her

hands holding one of her legs up high in the air

as she went round and round. Skating out of the

spin, it was time for another two

jumps, one following straight

after the other. She was

perfect! Hello Kitty

had never seen Fifi skate

so well. She cheered

loudly – **go Fifi!**

Fifi skated into the final spiral, gliding on the ice on one skate, her other leg held high in the air behind her, her arms reaching back. But as she glided round, Hello Kitty saw something red glinting on the ice. It was a hair clip – it must have dropped out of one of the other competitor's hair! And it was just where Fifi was about to skate! **Oh no!**

Hello Kitty held her breath, hoping that Fifi would miss the spot. But just then Fifi's skate caught against the clip. Her foot wobbled, and she lost her balance. She tumbled to the ice, landing hard on her left ankle.

All of the Friendship Club gasped and Hello

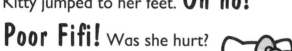
Kitty jumped to her feet. **Oh no!**
Poor Fifi! Was she hurt?

Fifi scrambled up. It looked like her ankle was hurting her, but she fixed a determined smile on her face. Hello Kitty could see she wasn't going to let a fall stop her from finishing her performance. She started to glide again and then as the music came to the end, she finished off with a fast spin. Round and round she went with her arms above her head, until, with perfect timing, she stopped on the last beat and smiled at the judges. She had done it! **Hooray!**

Everyone clapped and cheered — the
Friendship Club most of all — but Hello Kitty
couldn't help worrying as she saw Fifi skate off
the ice, being **very** gentle with her left leg
and looking very sore. Fifi had been so brave to
finish her routine but it looked like she was hurt.

Fifi went and sat in a special area with her coach to wait and see how she had done. The scores went up and Hello Kitty gasped – and started to clap and **cheer!** Even with her fall, Fifi had won! She had won the whole competition! But how was she? And was her ankle OK? Hello Kitty and the others felt very worried.

A little while later, Fifi's mum came back to find the Friendship Club. She had Fifi with her.

Her ankle was bandaged and she was using

a crutch to walk. She looked very unhappy

and sore.

Tammy and Hello Kitty *ran* to hug her.

What was the matter? Fifi's mum said they were

going to have to go to hospital to have her

ankle looked at, just in case. Fifi wailed loudly —
what if it was broken?

The Friendship Club looked at each other
as Fifi burst into tears. The school play was in
three days time! If she'd broken her ankle, how
could she **possibly** take part?

Fifi's mum drove them all back to Hello

Kitty's house so that she could take Fifi to

hospital. On the way, Hello Kitty tried to

comfort Fifi. She said she was sure Fifi could

still play Clara – even on crutches! Miss Davey

would find a way to change the play so she didn't have to dance. But Fifi shook her head — that would ruin the play, and she didn't want that. She would rather someone else took the part. It would need to be someone who knew the play really well though....

Someone – Tammy pointed out suddenly – who already knew the lines.

Dear Daniel nodded. Someone who knew all the dances too...

The Friendship Club **ALL** looked at Hello Kitty.

Hello Kitty suddenly realised what they were getting at. SHE knew the lines, didn't she? She didn't know all the dances though...

Fifi told her that it didn't matter – she could teach Hello Kitty the dances she didn't know! If they could get Miss Davey to agree she could take the part, then Fifi would help her as much as she could. She looked

at Hello Kitty. If she couldn't do it herself,

then there was no one else she would rather

see play Clara than Hello Kitty. Would she

do it? *Please?* Fifi looked at Hello Kitty

hopefully.

Hello Kitty gave a small smile. If Fifi really

couldn't do it and Miss Davey agreed, then of

course she would! She didn't want to let anyone down – especially not her friends. But first they needed to wait and see what the hospital said about Fifi's ankle...

The news from the hospital was a little better than expected. Fifi hadn't broken her ankle, only sprained it. But she **definitely** wouldn't be able to be in the show because she had to rest it.

The next morning, the Friendship Club went to see Miss Davey and told her what had happened. Miss Davey was very concerned when she heard about Fifi, but she quickly agreed that

Hello Kitty taking over the part was the perfect solution. If Fifi and her friends could show Hello Kitty the dances, and she could learn all the lines, then everything would be OK. The school play could definitely go ahead. **Phew!**

Hello Kitty had never worked so hard in her life! Mama and Mimmy took over

finishing off the costumes while she *practised* and *practised* the scenes and dances with Fifi, Tammy and Dear Daniel. She went to sleep thinking about her lines and dreamed about the dances all night long! She was so thankful to everyone for helping her.

By the evening before the play, Hello Kitty was starting to feel more confident. She had learned all her lines; she had danced all the steps. There wasn't **anything** more she could do, and she and Fifi were taking a rest after her final practice. And right now, she had one more favour to ask of Fifi...

Fifi was surprised as Hello Kitty pulled out
her letter to Santa. She had thought they had all
sent theirs off, but Hello Kitty explained that she
hadn't finished hers as she still needed to cut
some things! Would Fifi please help?

Fifi smiled. **Of course** she would!

And so the two girls looked at everything
on the list, and talked about what Hello Kitty
really wanted for Christmas. They
talked and talked, and drew and stuck stickers
on it, and by the time they had finished it was
all decided…

The Big Night

Hello Kitty stood in the wings at the side of the stage. She peered out from behind the curtains, butterflies fizzing in her tummy. The Christmas play hadn't even started and already she was full of nerves!

Hello Kitty could see her
parents sitting in the front row.
Grandpa and Grandma were with
them, too, with Fifi and her parents
sitting next to them. Hello Kitty gave
her friend a little **wave** from

behind the curtain. Fifi waved
back before crossing her fingers
and holding them up to wish Hello
Kitty luck. Then, Miss Davey called for
quiet, the music started and the curtain
went up. It was time for the play to begin!

Hello Kitty ran out on to the still dark stage and everyone took their places. The big Christmas tree had been moved on to the stage and looked as pretty as a picture with fairy lights twinkling and sparkling in the darkness. The costumes all looked **amazing** – just like Hello Kitty had imagined them. The show started with Hello Kitty as Clara and Timmy as her little brother Fritz, opening their Christmas presents! Clara opened the one with the nutcracker before finally settling down to sleep on stage. The Mouse King appeared and then Clara woke up to dance.

Scene after scene followed
until Hello Kitty found herself
in the Land of Sweets. Dancers in
brown tights and leotards spun to the music
before more dancers came on to a flute chorus
– they were played by Mimmy and her friends.

Hello Kitty waited as even more

dancers dressed as Russian

dolls danced on next, to the

sound of drums. It was so

exciting!

Now it was the turn of the Sugar Plum Fairy,

before Hello Kitty would come on again for the

last scene.

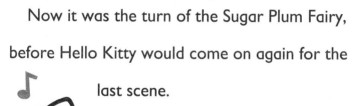

Finally, the Sugar Plum

Fairy danced off the stage

as Hello Kitty and Dear

Daniel took their places

for the last dance. They

danced across the stage

together, spinning and twirling and singing,

before Hello Kitty finally settled down to her

pretend-sleep. Then she gave a big yawn as

she pretended to wake up, clutching a little

crown in her hands. The curtain fell to the

sound of everyone cheering and clapping loudly!

Hooray!

After the final bow, Hello Kitty skipped off
the stage, pink with happiness. Her parents and
Mimmy were already waiting for her. She gave
them all a **big** hug. The Friendship Club were
there too and they all crowded
around as they told her
and Dear Daniel
how brilliant they
had been.

Hello Kitty
beamed. It had been
so much fun! She was so
grateful to everyone for helping her, especially
Fifi. She would never have been able to step into

the part without her help. And, she said, the last

few weeks had made her learn something really

important about Christmas.

Everyone wanted to know what that was, so

Hello Kitty explained. It had come to her when

she'd been taking
things off her
Christmas
list with
Fifi, just the
night before.
As they were

talking and working together, Hello Kitty had

realised that there was so much more to life

than presents. What was **really** important

was having good friends who were there for

you through thick and thin.

All her friends and family smiled. Fifi smiled

most of all, and announced that she thought it

called for a new friendship club rule — that the real joy of Christmas was not getting presents but being with your friends. Because:

Having a good friend is like getting a present every day!

Everyone loved it! Hello Kitty hugged her friends, before Mimmy turned and pointed excitedly out of the window. Little blobs of

white, like candyfloss, were starting to settle

on the window sills outside.

It had started to **SNOW** – and just in

time for Christmas! The perfect ending to the

perfect day.

Hello Kitty twirled around. Merry Christmas everyone!

Merry Christmas and a Happy New Year!

The end

Hello Kitty and her friends are setting up

a Christmas Party – and want you to join in!

Turn over the page for your

Christmas activities and fun.

HELLO KITTY
The Christmas Party

After the excitement of school is finally over
for Christmas, Hello Kitty and the
Friendship Club have one more thing to do.
They're having a sleepover at Hello Kitty's
house tomorrow, and have decided to have a party!
But not just any party – a Friendship Club
Christmas Party! Hooray!
On the following pages, you'll find instructions on
how to do everything for your very own Christmas
Party, from decorating your tree to making yummy
Christmas snacks for you and all your friends.

**Have fun – and
Merry Christmas!**

Christmas Tree Decorations

You can make your Christmas tree sparkle, just like the Friendship Club did at school! Follow the instructions here to decorate your tree for the most super Christmas ever.

You will need:

- Thin card
- Scissors
- String
- Coloured pens and pencils
- Glue
- Glitter and sequins to decorate

MAKE SURE YOU ASK MAMA OR PAPA TO HELP!

Christmas Stars

This is easy, but beautiful. Cut out star shapes from your card, and decorate them with glitter and sequins. Put a small hole in the top of each one, and thread them each on to a looped piece of string. Then hang them on your tree. Super-sparkly!

Snowflakes

You will need a piece of square card.

1 Fold the paper in half diagonally

2 Fold the triangle in half...

3 ...then fold one third to the front and one third to the back.

4 Trim the points off the bottom.

5 Cut into the folds, then open up your paper to reveal a beautiful snowflake!

Make a Hello Kitty Christmas Angel

Every Christmas tree needs a beautiful angel on top. And Hello Kitty will be the perfect angel for your tree!

MAKE SURE YOU ASK MAMA OR PAPA TO HELP!

You will need:

- A piece of white paper or thin card, A4 size
- Scissors
- Glue
- Glitter and coloured pencils and pens for decorating your angel.

1. Trace or copy the templates on to your piece of paper, and cut them out. If you have a big tree, you may need to make the pieces bigger – ask a grown-up to help you draw them.

2. Colour in the pieces and add glitter to Hello Kitty's wings. Make sure you wait for everything to dry before you start the next step.

3. Make a cone out of the angel's dress, and glue the sides together as marked.

4. Next, put a dab of glue in the middle of the wings, and attach them to your angel's back.

5. Ta da! You have a beautiful Hello Kitty Christmas Angel for the top of your tree!

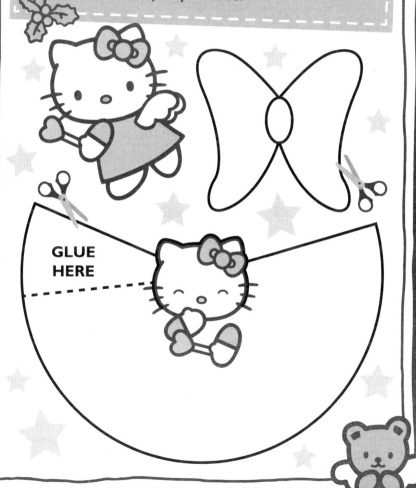

GLUE HERE

Chocolate-Chip Christmas Tree Cookies

Hello Kitty and Mama always bake these delicious cookies for Christmas, and they are always super-yummy, as well as being fun to make!

MAKE SURE YOU ASK MAMA OR PAPA TO HELP!

You will need:

- Some scissors and a piece of card
- 225g butter, softened
- 110g caster sugar
- 275g plain flour
- 125g of milk chocolate chips
- A large bowl
- An electric mixer (or a wooden spoon and lots of arm power!)
- A flat baking tray
- A butter knife

(Makes 35 cookies)

Before you start, copy or trace this template on to some card, and ask a grown-up to cut it out to help you shape your cookies!

Method:

1. Ask a grown-up to turn on the oven to 180°C / Gas 4.

2. Cream the butter in a large bowl with your mixer or wooden spoon until it's soft. Add the sugar and beat until the mixture is light and fluffy.

3. Sift in the flour and mix everything together to form a dough. Use your hands to mix the chocolate chips through evenly.

4. Using your hands, roll the dough into balls each about the size of a golf ball, and squash them down flat. Put the Christmas Tree template on top of each of them, and have your grown-up helper cut around it with the butter knife.

5. Place your Christmas Tree cookies slightly apart on a baking tray. Bake them in the oven for 13-15 minutes or until they are a light golden brown and slightly firm on top.

6. Ask your grown-up helper to carefully transfer the cookies to a wire rack to cool.

Yummy! Hello Kitty loves to eat her cookies with a big glass of milk.

Fantastic frames for your friends!

A great Christmas gift can be a beautiful framed photo of you and your friends – made by you! Follow the instructions to make a gorgeous Christmas frame for them to treasure.

MAKE SURE YOU ASK MAMA OR PAPA TO HELP!

You will need:

- A photo or picture of you and your friends
- Two pieces of thick cardboard
- A Pencil
- A ruler
- Scissors
- A glue stick or some glue
- Coloured pens, glitter and cotton wool balls.
- A magnet or string / ribbon.

1. Put your photo or picture face down in the middle of your thick card, and draw around the outside of it with a pencil.

2. Add 6 cm to each side of the square or rectangle you have traced, and draw another one outside, around it. This will be the outside of your frame.

3. Draw a smaller rectangle or square inside the first one, 1cm smaller on each side. This will be the inside edge of your frame and will stop your picture falling out!

4. Cut around the outside rectangle, then put it on your second piece of cardboard and cut out another piece the same size. This will be the back of your frame.

5. Cut the smaller rectangle out from the middle of your first piece of card. This will be the front of your frame.

6. Now it's time to decorate the front of your frame! Since it's Christmas, why not do a snow scene? You can use cotton wool and glitter for the falling snow – and you can even add a snowman! Make sure it's nice and bright!

7. Once the front has dried, turn over your frame and use a little bit of glue to stick your picture so it shows through the window at the front.

8. The put a bigger line of glue around it, and use it to stick on the back of your frame!

9. And last of all, stick a magnet or ribbon to the back of the frame, so your friend can stick or hang it up!

Hooray! It's a super-snowy frame to give as a present to a friend! Now, you just need to wrap it up... turn over the page for wrapping paper ideas!

Fifi

Wrap it up!

If you want to give a really personal present at Christmas, why not make your own wrapping paper? It's an inexpensive way to show how much thought you've put into a present – and is fun to make too! Make sure you ask a grown-up to help you with any cutting.

Collage crazy

You will need scissors, glue, old magazines, plain paper to decorate and some glitter.

Method:

1. Cut out the pictures you want from your magazines, and glue them to your paper, making sure you leave space in between them for your glitter.

2. When you're happy with the amount of pictures, draw a line of glue between them all and sprinkle it with glitter. Shake or brush off any excess, and leave it to dry before wrapping your present.

Pretty potato prints

You will need plain paper to decorate, some potatoes, a knife, a pen and different coloured paints. Make sure you have a grown-up do any cutting with the knife for you!

Method:

1. Cut your potato in half, dry it on a tea towel, and draw the design you want on the flat side.

2. Have your grown-up helper score round your drawing with the knife and cut away the surrounding potato until your design is raised up.

3. Dip the design part of your potato in your paint, and use it to stamp your design on to the paper.

4. Repeat with as many colours or different designs as you want, and don't forget to let it dry before wrapping your presents!

Make your own Christmas cards

Making your own Christmas cards is easy and fun, and will mean a lot to the person you give it to. All you need is some stiff paper, scissors, glue, cotton wool balls, coloured pens and pencils, and decorations like glitter and ribbon to give your cards the perfect finishing touches!

Here are some ideas to get you started!

Hello Kitty Card

You can make this card extra special by making Hello Kitty's Bow out of real ribbon, and gluing it on!

Snow Scene card

Cotton wool balls can make a snowy card just super! Colour in your card first and then stick them on where snow or smoke would go.

Window Wonderland!

Ask your grown-up helper to cut a window in the front of your card, and then draw a Christmas scene you can see inside, through the window. Make sure you leave some space at the bottom for your message too.

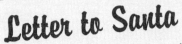

Letter to Santa

Hello Kitty and her friends have all written their letters to Santa, and sent them off to the North Pole! Copy the template on the opposite page on to a blank piece of paper, using the tips below.

Hello Kitty Tips:

- Think about what you really want for Christmas before you write your letter. Remember what Hello Kitty found out – sometimes the best present of all isn't one that you can buy!

- Decorate your letter to make it stand out! Santa gets lots of letters every year so it's always nice if one of them looks extra special. You can use drawings, glitter, or even stickers!

- Check to make sure you have everything right! You can ask a grown-up to help you check your spelling, and you can write out your letter more than once to make sure you haven't missed anything out, and have it all neat and tidy.

To Santa Claus,
The North Pole.

Dear Santa,
I hope you and the reindeer and Mrs Clause are happy and having a Merry Christmas so far! What I want most for Christmas is:

_____

_____

_____

_____

_____

Don't work too hard this Christmas, and give my best wishes to Rudolph!

Love from,

XXXX

It's time to Party!

Now that you have everything you need, it's time to party with all your friends for Christmas. Put on some Christmas carols, grab a cookie and chill out! You deserve it after all your hard work. And Hello Kitty has one final message for you before we say good night...

Thanks so much for coming to the Friendship Club's very first Christmas Party, and for joining us in our first year together. There have been lots of adventures and we've all had a super time; I hope you have too! Have a very Merry Christmas and a Happy New Year – and look out for more books coming soon!

Love from

Hello Kitty
xxx

Turn the page for a sneak peek at

HELLO KITTY
and friends'

next adventure...

The TV Star

Hello Kitty sat at the top of the slide. She covered her eyes with both hands before sliding all the way down to the bottom, laughing and calling as she went. Wheeeeeeee! It was a sunny day and Hello Kitty couldn't think of anywhere she would rather be than in the park with her friends. Dear Daniel followed on behind and Tammy after that. They landed with a bump at the bottom. Now all that they needed was for Fifi to arrive at the park and complete the group!

The four of them were really good friends and together they made up the Friendship Club. They met to do all sorts of fun things like baking and dancing and painting. They were going to a meeting at Fifi's house that afternoon, only it was too nice to be inside right now so they had decided to go to the park first instead.

Hello Kitty looked across the grass to where her mama was sitting in the shade of the trees with Hello Kitty's twin sister, Mimmy, who was playing her flute.

Just then, Fifi arrived and saw them. She looked excited as she came running across the grass to join the rest of the Friendship Club. She had a scrapbook under one arm and was waving a piece of paper in the other. Hello Kitty called to Dear Daniel and Tammy to come over quickly. They ran with her to meet Fifi. She DID look very excited – what could she possibly have to tell them?

Fifi jumped up and down. She had just found out that she was going to be a TV presenter for a day!

How super! Everyone gasped, Hello Kitty high-fived her and Dear Daniel and Tammy said it was brilliant. Everyone wanted to ask Fifi

questions so she asked them all to slow down

so that she could answer them one at

a time.

Dear Daniel wanted to know what the show

was going to be about, so Fifi told him that it

was for Fun and Friendship – a programme

about family and friends.

Tammy wanted to know what Fifi had had to

do to become a presenter.

So Fifi told her all about how she had made a

friendship scrapbook. She had just been putting

it together for fun, but her mother had seen it

and sent it into the programme. They had liked

it so much they had asked her to go on to the show!

Hello Kitty asked what was in the scrapbook. Fifi told her that the first page was all about friendship and who her friends were, but then after that there were lots of different pages:

Birthdays

Special family moments

Travel with friends

Recipes

There were lots of glittery drawings and photos in it, and stickers too. It was beautiful!

They all started chattering at once, wondering what Fifi would have to do when she was presenting the programme, and Fifi said that she would just be presenting a short section where she would show the viewers how to make a friendship scrapbook of their own. It sounded like really good fun! Hooray!

Mama poured everyone a fizzy pink lemonade while they talked and talked, turning over the pages of Fifi's scrapbook. It had a purple cover and was decorated all over with little silver stars. Hello Kitty liked the birthdays' page best. Fifi had stuck in photos of them all and labeled them with their names, their dates of birth and some old birthday cards. Dear Daniel liked the page on travel where Fifi had put tickets from the different trips they had been on together. There was even an old concert ticket from when they had all gone to see the band the Fizzy Pops. Tammy liked the recipe for chocolate friendship muffins best. Yummy!

But the scrapbook wasn't quite finished, whispered Fifi – she wanted to put in more photos and make some more pages before she went on the show to talk about it, but she was running out of time! Filming for the programme was on Monday – just after the weekend. There wasn't long to put it all together…

Hello Kitty grinned. She knew exactly who could help – the Friendship Club, of course!

They could start that very afternoon.

Fifi grinned gratefully. The Friendship Club were the best!

Find out what happens next in...

Coming soon!

· A HELLO KITTY STORY ·

HELLO KITTY

and friends

The TV Star

Coming soon:

· A HELLO KITTY STORY ·

HELLO KITTY
and friends

The TV Star

Collect all of the Hello Kitty and Friends Stories!

The Friendship Club

The School Trip

The Summer Fair

The Pop Princess

The Wedding Day

The Beach Holiday

The Treasure Hunt

The Talent Show

The Christmas Present